The Byzantine Pineapple (Part 1)

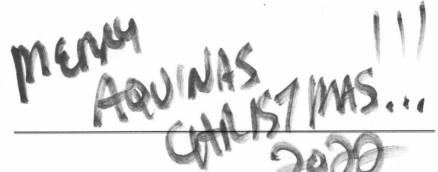

MERRY AQUINAS CHRISTMAS...!!! 2020

The Byzantine Pineapple
(Part 1)

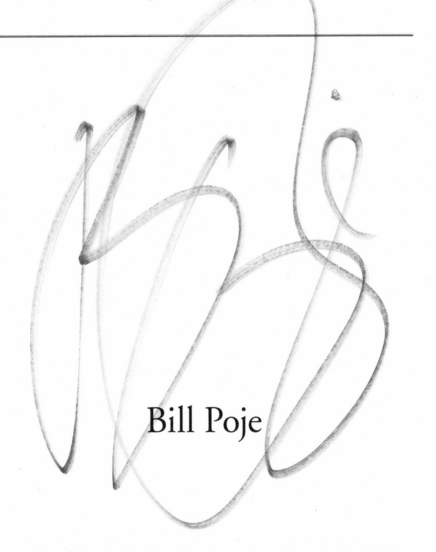

Bill Poje

Library of Congress Control Number:		2018911389
ISBN:	Hardcover	978-1-9845-5503-8
	Softcover	978-1-9845-5502-1
	eBook	978-1-9845-5550-2

Print information available on the last page.

Rev. date: 10/05/2018

To order additional copies of this book, contact:
Xlibris
1-888-795-4274
www.Xlibris.com
Orders@Xlibris.com
779516

This book is dedicated to all those who have or will wake up from The Matrix and who desire a new and improved Social-Economic-Legal-Political construct

CONTENTS

PART 1

What Is the Byzantine Pineapple?

Introduction: How Did This Text Come Into Existence? xi

Chapter 1   What Is the Byzantine Pineapple? 1
Chapter 2   About the Author...8
Chapter 3   How Do Current Socioeconomic Legal Political
             (SELP) Systems Work?..10
Chapter 4   The Structure of the Text..13

PART 2

Example of SELP System Failures

Chapter 5   Legal Systems: Who or What Is Legal, and How
             Is Legality Determined?..21
Chapter 6   Why Existing SELP Systems Are Doomed to Fail........30

PART 3

Design Parameters for Creating a New SELP System Design

Chapter 7   Defining Design Parameters for a New SELP
             System Design 39
Chapter 8   A New SELP System Design.......................................47
Chapter 9   Conclusion 64

Appendix A: Definitions Of The Flat Tax Formula........................67

PART 1

What Is the Byzantine Pineapple?

How Did This Text Come into Existence?

THIS TEXT IS the tenth revision of what was originally a fictional legal story created out of frustration to the legal challenges mounted against the (ironically named) Affordable Care Act (ACA) or Obamacare in the USA. The author is of the opinion that the legal argument approach to challenging ACA was completely misguided. The opinion of the author is that the individual mandate should have been challenged on the grounds that it creates an "existence tax" and that the framers of both the Declaration of Independence and the US Constitution would consider the imposition of any existence tax to be in direct violation of the concept of unalienable Rights to life, liberty, and the pursuit of happiness.

The author wrote revision 1. Upon reading the first draft, the author realized areas that are "legal argument flawed" based on existing Supreme Court rulings and that these issues needed to be addressed in the second revision. After creating the second revision, the author read the text and realized that this revision again had areas that are "legal argument flawed" based on existing Supreme Court rulings and that these issues needed to be addressed in the third revision. After writing and reading the third revision and coming to the same conclusion again, the author woke up from "The Matrix" and realized that there is no legal argument for independence that cannot be overruled by prior US Supreme Court rulings. In essence, the *system* is rigged against *independence*. The system is rigged against freedom of life, liberty, and the pursuit of happiness.

The system is rigged by the existence of hundreds of thousands of arcane rules and laws and regulations that are impossible for any citizen to know, yet any single one of these hundreds of thousands of arcane rules and laws and regulations can selectively be used to prosecute and persecute a citizen who falls out of favor with the state. These hundreds of thousands of arcane rules and laws and regulations comprise a Byzantine construct.

This Byzantine construct of hundreds of thousands of arcane rules and laws and regulations all end up taking capital from the citizens via taxation, fees, etc., and the capital is redistributed to those who have government influence and friends. Those on the inside eat the fruit of the Byzantine pineapple.

The solution, then, became one of following the laws of nature. In nature, there is constant change and evolution. It is time to evolve the systems of governance. The existing Byzantine pineapple system needs to evolve to the new system—a new system without a Byzantine pineapple construct.

The trick is envisioning and creating an evolution of the existing system so that the new system replaces the Byzantine pineapple system with a simpler socioeconomic legal political (SELP) system that treats citizens in a more equitable manner. The result of envisioning and creating an evolution of the existing system is this text.

CHAPTER 1

What Is the Byzantine Pineapple?

I T IS SAID that the definition of *insanity* is "doing the same thing over and over again, expecting a different result." It is also said that the only people you know are sane are those let out of the insane asylum because they are the only people with a certificate of sanity; you don't know about the rest of the people. Think about those two thoughts and look around you. There are plenty of insane people walking around because they keep yelling and fighting which of the right or the left is a political system that will permanently solve the issues of hunger and housing and health care for the citizens of countries.

This is not to say that the world is not in a better place because of the efforts of the right and the left. Rather, the issue is that both systems have run their course and they need an upgrade to a new system that melds the good pieces of both sides together while eliminating the corruption that dominates the current socioeconomic legal political (SELP) systems. Like the early versions of *The Matrix*, the failures of the existing SELP systems have created an escalating probability of disaster. Like *The Matrix*, there is a need to create a new SELP revision level to address the needs of the growing global human population.

There are seven-billion-plus humans on planet earth. These seven-billion-plus people are managed by 196 countries (plus odd authoritarian entities such as the United Nations or the Vatican or the Palestinian Authority). Each country/entity has its own SELP system. Each SELP system appears to have embedded system-designed corruption that will never be eliminated by adding more patchwork laws on more patchwork laws. To eliminate the corruption, there needs to be a new SELP system design. To believe otherwise fits the definition of *insanity*.

Currently, there is a large schism globally between those on the left and the right, driven by those who promote their political parties' form of SELP as a way to govern citizens. Curiously, though, there are four common social goals between not only the right and the left but also independents that really seem to cover the vast majority of political differences:

1. Provide an income to each citizen.
2. Provide health care (not health insurance) to each citizen.
3. Provide some form of housing to each citizen.
4. Treat citizens equally regardless of age or gender or race or religion or other dividing factors.

Ask yourself this question: Which political party entity has a SELP system that is known to 100 percent *cost-effectively*

1. provide an income to each citizen?
2. provide health care (not health insurance) to each citizen?
3. provide some form of housing to each citizen?
4. treat citizens equally regardless of age or gender or race or religion or other dividing factors?

The answer is *no* political party entity has a SELP system that is known to 100 percent cost-effectively accomplish the four goals outlined above. The definition of *insanity* is "doing the same thing over and over again, expecting a different result." Since the end result of following the existing parties will be the same failures to accomplish the four primary goals, why continue to follow the existing parties?

This, in a nutshell, is what *The Byzantine Pineapple* is about. The SELP systems governing humans are very *Byzantine* in nature, as every year, more and more laws are passed that increasingly make the governmental systems more and more Byzantine in nature. Annually, though, taxes are collected. Those who get the tax money are those inside the *pineapple* of government dole, while those outside the *Byzantine pineapple* get deterred by the outer defense mechanisms of the pineapple.

The text *The Byzantine Pineapple* is about a new SELP system design that restructures the existing SELP system into a new system that cost-effectively achieves four goals:

1. Provide an income to each citizen.
2. Provide health care (not health insurance) to each citizen.
3. Provide some form of housing to each citizen.
4. Treat citizens equally regardless of age or gender or race or religion or other dividing factors.

Globally, there is a growth of political independents—citizens independent from the existing political parties in their countries. More and more people globally see the political corruption going on with the existing SELP systems, and they are leaving the main political parties in droves as they seek a new SELP systems solution.

Common sense indicates to the independents that such a SELP system does not yet exist. So logically, until such a system is designed and agreed upon for implementation, the existing systems will continue to produce flawed results that will have some successes but are overwhelmingly failing because of the inherent system flaws. The inherent system flaws exist because

a. changing leadership isn't going to solve the inherent system flaws,
b. putting in term limits isn't going to solve the inherent system flaws, and
c. making governments bigger and bigger with more Byzantinely worded, massive, omnibus bills that no one is thoroughly reading before voting on is not going to solve the system flaws.

Redesigning the system to address the system flaws is necessary to solve them. But to successfully redesign and implement system reform requires first having a comprehensive SELP system plan.

The author of this text is an American. This text uses the American governmental system to present the inherent system flaws in the current

SELP systems. However, it is the opinion of the author that the same inherent flaws in the American SELP systems exist in the rest of the approximate two hundred different governmental SELP systems around the globe. There are certain common inherent SELP system construct flaws in all existing global systems that prevent achieving the four common goals.

Countries are run by either a permanent dictatorial cabal or have some form of free elections that put people into power for some length of time. No matter what system exists, there will always be some groups that must be the ruling power. This is exhibited in nature with all the various ant colonies. There is always a queen up top ruling over all the various classes in the ant colony. Someone always rules. The trick is constructing a SELP system that actually achieves the four stated SELP system goals while also establishing control over the leadership by the populace.

If a person is a citizen of a dictatorial cabal, then the citizen is subject to the whims of those in power, and the first rule of those in power is to keep power as long as possible while the events of the world change around them. If a person is a citizen of a freely elected government, then the citizen is subject to the whims of those in power too. Ergo, the way to design a new SELP system is to construct the system so that the citizens are more subject to consistent SELP system application instead of constant change based on the whims of those in power.

Regardless of the country one is a citizen of, the probability is that those in power have succeeded prior rulers / elected leaders. What occurs with the new power structure is that it creates more laws on top of all the laws that have already been established by prior power structures. These legal layers on top of decades or centuries of legal layers have created a Byzantine system.

The Byzantine system layers are like the layers of the pineapple. Inside, the Byzantine pineapple is the tasty fruit, but unless one has the machete to get at the fruit, then one does not get to partake in the feast. Only those inside get to partake of the Byzantine pineapple.

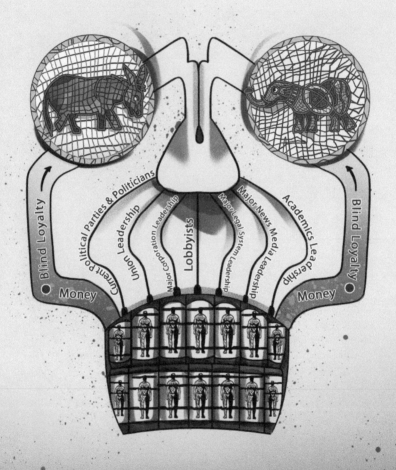

Asleep in the Matrix

Our side's slogans are coolest.
Our side is better at making fun of the other side; we are snarkier.

Our side has the plan to salvation
The other side is the path to the destruction of Earth

Our side's tax plan will solve everything
The other side's tax plan only enriches their supporters.

Our economic plan will give provide everyone with "good paying jobs"
The other side only enriches themselves while killing jobs and income.

Our health insurance plan will take care of everyone at low cost.
The other side will kill people with their plan.

Our housing plan will eliminate homelessness.
The other side will kill the homeless.

Every day is a new crisis for you to panic over.
Every new crisis needs more money to solve.

There is something wrong with you.
You are obese or too thin, too ugly or too beautiful, too dumb or too smart, etc.

You need to feel guilty about who you are and about how you are destroying the Earth.
The way to atone for your sins is to give our side more money!

Racism, Sexism, Ageism, terrorists, violent radicals, etc., are everywhere.
Hate and distrust everyone....especially "the other side."

The other side is "racist".
Our side is not "racist."

There are not enough laws.
More and more and more and more laws are always needed.

Passing massive omnibus bills that no one is reading at the threat of government shutdown is just good politics.
There is no other way.

The government mess is all because of the other side.
Our side is virginal.

You are either 100% with our side or you are the problem.

There is no other way.

CHAPTER 2

About the Author

THE READERS WILL undoubtedly ask themselves at some point, What qualifies the author to be believed for a new SELP system design? The answer is that the author has both education and experience, qualifying him to be able to opine on the subject with validity. A small sample of a lifetime of work and learning is noted below.

From the fall of 1984 to the spring of 1988, the author completed 115 undergraduate school hours and sixty graduate school credit hours. In essence, the author completed both undergraduate and graduate school in four years' time.

The undergraduate degree was a joint accounting / business administration degree and an MBA that was conferred in the concentration of finance and operations management. Between undergraduate and graduate schools, the author completed twenty hours of information systems coursework (enough for a minor) as well as completing or auditing all coursework required for an MBA concentration in marketing.

During graduate school, the author took international finance and economics taught by Dewey Daane, who was appointed to the Board of Governors of the Federal Reserve Board by John F. Kennedy in November 1963 and served on the board until 1974. Mr. Daane was instrumental in the ending of the Bretton Woods Agreement that established the gold standard. When Wall Street crashed in 1987, the *Wall Street Journal* immediately had a front-page article by Mr. Daane, concerning the latest ongoing market crash.

The author spent eight years working for a global Japanese manufacturing firm that produces both automotive and nonautomotive products. The author was responsible for managing the standard cost system and all governmental regulatory reporting in terms of NAFTA, AALA, CAFE, and product marking and labeling.

The author was also in charge of product estimating. The author was instrumental in changing an annually financial-losing company for nineteen out of twenty years into an annually profitable corporation. The products estimated were primarily push-pull cables (e.g., transmission cables, brake cables, and steering cables). And the author was responsible for at least 25 percent of all original equipment manufacturing push-pull cables sold annually in the USA.

The author also lived in both Grand Cayman and Grand Bahama Islands during which time the author was the financial controller for the largest exporter out of the Bahamas. The author installed a full ERP / accounting system, financial report writer, payroll system, biometric time and attendance system while also cleaning up the corporation's financials. The author also envisioned, designed, and started implementation of a now fully functional data system that collects data from the Bahamian manufacturing facilities' PLCs (for a factory that operates 24-7-365 or never-ceasing operations) and transfers the data to the ERP / accounting system as well as to management.

The author has accomplished a lot more and has a variety of products that have been successfully market-tested and are ready for global production. The author is of the opinion that this lifetime of accomplishment qualifies him to design a new SELP system.

CHAPTER 3

How Do Current Socioeconomic Legal Political (SELP) Systems Work?

W ITH RESPECT TO SELP systems in the USA and many other countries around the globe, there are elections, and the election winning regime does the following:

1. Pass a bunch of laws, adding laws on existing laws.
2. Cut or raise taxes.
3. Cut or add social welfare programs.

Obviously, there are foreign policy issues and other issues that also occur, but for the most part, these actions occur. These are three established reasons why the SELP systems will ultimately fail:

1. The continuous stream of new laws enacted continually add Byzantine layers to existing Byzantine SELP systems that have basically made all citizens illegal in some way, shape, or form just by the citizens leading their normal lives, while also making criminal activities legal.

   What eventually ends up occurring is a breakdown of law because the common citizens see lots of common citizens that they feel they should be free from being incarcerated and having their lives ruined unnecessarily due to ambiguous application of laws. Simultaneously, the common citizens see many powerful people commit what they feel are obvious crimes, and the powerful people go free. For the citizenship, the philosophical construct of what is legal and illegal is gone.

2. All the tax changes every year create an unstable, disruptive system that has no endgame and no real purpose. However, all the tax changes establish and pit different classes of citizens against one another rather than treating all citizens equally.

   What ends up occurring is that all sorts of arcane taxes are continually created with rules designed to benefit certain parts of the populace at the expense of other parts of the populace. But since the taxation system is so convoluted, the citizenship really can't tell what is truly going on with taxes. All the common citizens know is that there are base tax rates and tax credits and base income deductions, but there is no way for them to have any confidence that they are being treated equitably in relationship to others. This leads to a belief on the part of much of the common citizenship—that they are getting screwed as their tax dollars are unfairly given to others.

3. All the social welfare programs exist to spend tax dollars while never existing for an endgame. However, all the social welfare programs establish and pit different classes of citizens against one another rather than treating all citizens equally.

   What ends up occurring is that the social welfare programs rarely cease. Instead, they continue to grow in size to be paid more, and there will be more government employees to manage the programs while providing less benefit to the common taxpaying citizenship. This leads to class anger between those paying for the social welfare programs and those receiving from the social welfare programs.

The above three issues establish the parameters for a new SELP system:

1. A system design that clearly defines for all citizens what is conceptually legal and illegal
2. A system design that has a stable tax system that treats citizens equally.
3. A system design of social welfare programs that is streamlined and treats all citizens equally

CHAPTER 4

The Structure of the Text

THE BYZANTINE PINEAPPLE is intended to be a simplistic presentation of a new SELP system and specifically a macroeconomic formula that is a more equitable government management system that can be ultimately understood by high school-- educated people globally. The opinion is that common people will get it once the plan is presented to them. The opinion is that once people get it, they will support the plan.

Current political parties and politicians, union leadership, major corporation leadership, lobbyists, major legal system leadership, major news media leadership, and academics leadership won't like the plan. Why? Because the Byzantine system that they have created enriches those at the top of these echelons at the expense of the common populace while also perpetuating their power grasp over the common populace.

These echelons won't state their objection so bluntly. They will proclaim that the SELP system proposals in this text and, specifically, the macroeconomic flat tax formula contained herein are worthless because some universities and federal agencies haven't developed and blessed the SELP system proposals backed up by arcane mathematical formulations understood by only a few. Ask yourself this question: If the echelons really know what they proclaim to know, then why are all the current SELP systems continuously such a jumbled mess?

The fact of the matter is that the echelons are all enriching themselves at the expense of the common populace because of the current Byzantine SELP systems that they created and perpetuated! Follow the Benjamins. The echelons get paid to perpetuate the current SELP systems.

This text is Part 1 of 3 planned texts:

1. This version of *The Byzantine Pineapple* Part 1 has 1 part. An abridged version is also available. The Abridged Version only contains the first half noted below. This version is the low cost version for mass consumption.

   The first half deals with Systems Analysis and Systems Design of the existing SELP systems. The Systems Design segment presents a brand new Flat Tax Macroeconomic formula that can be used at any level of government and by any government on the planet.

   The second half of the text presents the Corporation X Business Plan. This plan is a 10 year $6 billion dollar global sales vision that creates products as well as a production and marketing corporation that can be used to take The Byzantine Pineapple to the Common People around the globe...while greatly profiting those who choose to invest in Corporation X.

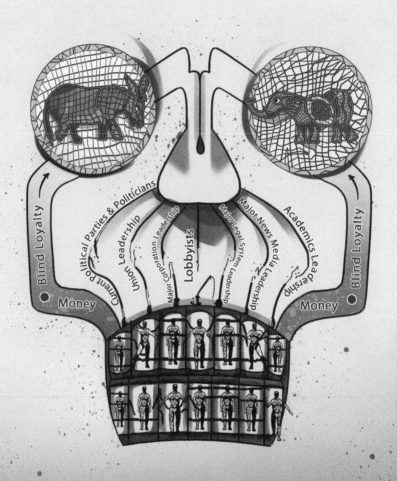

Waking from the Matrix

~~Our side's slogans are coolest.~~
~~Our side is better at making fun of the other side; we are snarkier.~~
SLOGAN'S AND MAKING FUN OF PEOPLE ARE NOT PLANS IMPROVING SOCIETY!

~~Our side has the plan to salvation~~
~~The other side is the path to the destruction of Earth~~
NEITHER SIDE HAS A CLEARLY DEFINED PLAN FOR THE FUTURE!

~~Our side's tax plan will solve everything~~
~~The other side's tax plan only enriches their supporters.~~
BOTH SIDES ALWAYS MODIFY TAXES TO BUY VOTES!

~~Our economic plan will give provide everyone with "good paying jobs"~~
~~The other side only enriches themselves while killing jobs and income.~~
THERE 70,000,000+ UNEMPLOYED PEOPLE IN THE USA.
IT IS IMPOSSIBLE TO CREATE 70,000,000+ JOBS!

~~Our health insurance plan will take care of everyone at low cost.~~
~~The other side will kill people with their plan.~~
INSURANCE SYSTEMS ARE COSTLY AND TREAT PEOPLE UNEQUALLY.
IF "HEALTH CARE" IS A RIGHT OF ALL CITIZENS THEN THERE IS NO NEED FOR A HEALTH INSURANCE SYSTEM!

~~Our housing plan will eliminate homelessness.~~
~~The other side will kill the homeless.~~
NEITHER SIDE HAS A VIABLE PLAN TO ELIMINATE HOMELESSNESS!

~~Every day is a new crisis for you to panic over.~~
~~Every new crisis needs more money to solve.~~
THE STORIES OF CRISIS ARE BEING PLANTED TO GET MONEY!
THERE IS NO GREAT CRISIS!

~~There is something wrong with you.~~
~~You are obese or too thin, too ugly or too beautiful, too dumb or too smart, etc.~~
JUST BECAUSE WE ARE ALL DIFFERENT DOESN'T MEAN THERE IS SOMETHING WRONG WITH YOU!
YOU ARE WHO YOU ARE...AND NO DRUGS/PRODUCTS/ETC. WILL CHANGE THAT!

You need to feel guilty about who you are and about how you are destroying the Earth.

The way to atone for your sins is to give our side more money!

JUST BECAUSE SOMEONE CLAIMS THEIR CHARITY/CAUSE IS DOING "GOOD" DOESN'T MEAN THAT IT IS.

QUIT FEELING GUILTY BECAUSE SOME ECHELON TELLS YOU TO FEEL GUILT!

Racism, Sexism, Ageism, terrorists, violent radicals, etc., are everywhere.

Hate and distrust everyone…..especially "the other side."

IF YOU ADD UP ALL THE REPORTED ACTS OF HATE IN THE USA IT ADDS UP TO 0.0000000% OF THE 300+ MILLION PEOPLE IN THE USA!

THAT MEANS THAT 300+ MILLION OF US CITIZENS GET ALONG WELL EVERY SINGLE DAY!

The other side is "racist".

Our side is not "racist."

RACISM MEANS MAKING DECISIONS BY RACE!

THE BIGGEST RACISTS ARE THE POLITICAL PARTIES, GOVERNMENTS, MAJOR CORPORATIONS, NEWS MEDIA AND EDUCATIONAL INSTUTUTIONS!

WHY?

BECAUSE THEY SEGREGATE AND MAKE DECISIONS BASED SOLELY UPON RACE!

There are not enough laws.

More and more and more and more laws are always needed.

ALL CITIZENS ARE NOW ILLEGAL BECAUSE THERE ARE SO MANY LAWS NOW THAT IT IS IMPOSSIBLE NOT TO BE ILLEGAL.

LESS, BETTER DEFINED LAWS ARE NEEDED!

Passing massive omnibus bills that no one is reading at the threat of government shutdown is just good politics.

There is no other way.

MASSIVE LEGISLATION WRITTEN BY LOBBYISTS AND PASSED WITHOUT ANYONE REALLY READING THE BILLS WRITTEN SO VAGUELY THAT THE COURT SYSTEM MUST CONTINUALLY RULE UPON THE VAGUE LEGISLATION SHOULD BE LABELED AS "CRIMINBUS BILLS."

THERE ARE OTHER WAYS.

The government mess is all because of the other side.

Our side is virginal.

BOTH SIDES HAVE CREATED THE MESS OF GOVERNMENT!

BOTH SIDES ARE RESPONSIBLE!

You are either 100% with our side or you are the problem.

There is no other way.

BLIND ADHERENCE TO FALSE PROMISES OF POLITICAL PARTIES IS THE PROBLEM!

THERE ARE OTHER WAYS!

PART 2

Example of SELP System Failures

CHAPTER 5

Legal Systems
Who or What Is Legal, and
How Is Legality Determined?

I N THE USA, it is seemingly impossible to determine what actions are criminal or not criminal. This is because there is no clear definition of what determines what is legal and what is illegal. To explain this further, the author chooses to tie together four seemingly independent legal examples:

1. Troubled Asset Relief Program (TARP)
2. Affordable Care Act (ACA a.k.a. Obamacare) vis-à-vis the Congressional Budget Office (CBO)
3. Personal-choice freedom: legal/illegal substances as well as vices and seat belts
4. Civil asset forfeiture and economic eminent domain

Troubled Asset Relief Program (TARP)

TARP was developed to bail out a variety of companies that stood to enter bankruptcy due to a combination of fraud and just plain bad decision-making. All of a sudden, seemingly overnight, both the Republicans and the Democrats proclaimed that the USA and other countries around the globe *must* pass the bailouts. Otherwise, there would be a global economic crash.

Obviously, these declarations were made without the politicians or the news media even reading or comprehending the very open-ended TARP legislation. The Matrix program told the politicians and the news media to tell citizens that TARP *must* happen, and they repeated what they were told to repeat. It was amazing how the news media and the politicians all said the same thing every day. It was almost like they all received a daily email telling everyone how to speak and act in front of the cameras.

This bailout was sold as what could only be described as trickle-down socialism. The social benefit of bailing out the corrupt corporation- or government-created regulatory system would be of greater social benefit versus letting the bankruptcy courts take over and settle things.

What really happened with TARP was that a bunch of very wealthy and powerful people (and their entourages) stood to lose massive amounts of wealth due to their bad money management decisions. They didn't want to do that. So they cooked up a scheme like that of *Chicken Little*'s "The sky is falling" with their paid-for politicians and media to proclaim that they must be bailed out or the economic system would collapse and the four horsemen of the economic apocalypse would ride the land. So the wealthy and powerful got their losses paid for by the governments that work for them. They didn't end up losing money (and, inherently, power).

And then to help pay for TARP, interest rates were lowered to 0 percent so the banks could borrow at 0 percent and lend at higher rates, guaranteeing positive cash flow. And the corporations were gifted tax credits to benefit the newly appointed White House–selected ownership. How convenient!

Who pays for this scheme? *Taxpayers!* This magic TARP legislation seemingly appeared overnight and put the taxpayers on the hook for the losses. Even better for the rich and powerful, the whole scheme was legal because ruling governments around the globe said it was legal. The issues that global governments saying that TARP's legal doesn't mean that TARP wasn't criminal.

Affordable Care Act (ACA a.k.a. Obamacare) vis-à-vis the Congressional Budget Office (CBO)

Soon after TARP, the USA passed the ACA, even though, obviously, no politicians or news media actually read the legislation. To pass the legislation, the politicians had the legislation financially scored by the Congressional Budget Office (CBO) as being deficit neutral with all sorts of other hokey proclamations about how many Americans would now be insured due to ACA. Using a little common sense, one can understand just how hokey the ACA sales job by the CBO was.

After the passage of ACA, there was subsequent rules and regulations issued. There is no one definitive source that can state how many regulations were attributable to ACA, but the number appears to be between five thousand and fifteen thousand rules and regulations issued. Each rule and regulation had a cost impact associated with it.

Ask yourself this question: How could the CBO have scored the cost impact of all the subsequent five-thousand-plus rules and regulations that came out after ACA passed? The answer is that there is no way CBO could have scored the cost impact of all the added rules and regulations!

This demonstrates how ludicrous the current SELP is while also epitomizing the Byzantine pineapple. This is a Byzantine system of government bureaucracies passing unread legislation using known phony numbers to justify passing the unread legislation—legislation that creates more and more Byzantine layers of government, as well as law, rules, and regulations.

Make sure you understand what this means! This means that the CBO is useless. It 100 percent fails at the task it was created to achieve. Yet simultaneously, the CBO scoring is a major lynchpin of passing legislation (Legislation being voted into law that few, if any, politicians have read and understand) in the United States! The political parties have created a system whereby useless proclamations are used to justify passing legislation! In the private industry, that is considered fraud. In the political industry, it is all legal to commit such fraud!

At the same time, there is now an *existence tax* on the citizen's head. If the citizen *exists*, the citizen is now subjected to a health insurance tax just for existing. If the citizen doesn't either pay directly for health insurance or pay a tax, then the citizen is a *criminal* (!).

Ask yourself this question: Do you think an existence tax is what the signers of the Declaration of Independence had in mind when they established the freedom to pursue life, liberty, and happiness? The author certainly doesn't and is of the opinion that the vast majority of citizens of countries around the globe agree.

Personal-Choice Freedom: Legal/Illegal Substances as well as Vices and Seat Belts

Simultaneously, the surveillance technology of the US government has grown by leaps and bounds. The citizen basically has to assume that every single action or word uttered is being recorded somewhere and can be used against them at any point in time.

The failure is that as human history has shown, humans like to engage in vices and personally dangerous behavior, and the legal system has outlawed the personal activity that people like to engage in while letting others get away with the same behavior because under some form of logic, one form of the same behavior is legal and the other is illegal. This allows the all-surveilling state unfettered reign to lock up and besmirch selective lives without really a concept of what being a criminal is. *The Trial* has begun.

This means that many citizens can't truly enjoy freedom of personal choice—a.k.a. life, liberty, and the pursuit of happiness—because the all-surveilling state has constructed a SELP system with selective prosecution. It is the selective prosecution that drives wedges into society because citizens find themselves at war with the state over issues of what being a criminal is.

There are five primary categories that need a SELP resolution, because no matter whether the activities are legal or illegal, there will always be millions of citizens engaging in the categories. A certain percentage of citizens will always partake in

1. using recreational substance of all sorts of natural and synthetic products,
2. trading money for sexual activity,
3. gambling,
4. engaging in personally dangerous physical activity for a thrill, and
5. aborting.

There has never been a time in recorded human history where a percentage of the human population hasn't engaged in the five behaviors above. Whether it offends one's personal morals or not, people are going to engage in these behaviors. Why is the SELP system structured to ruin people's lives by criminalizing them for being human?

Why is it criminal for the common citizens to be jailed for their vices, to be denied employment for their vices, and to have degrading marks put by the government on their personal records when the rich and powerful rarely get convicted for the same behavior? Look at the population of jailed drug offenders in the USA, and it is obvious that more common citizens are being jailed versus wealthy citizens.

Why is it illegal for common citizens to enjoy some vices while it is legal for those controlling the politicians and media to get a TARP-sized bailout? The bailouts occurred because the rich and powerful were too busy enjoying their vices rather than managing their investments.

It is only illegal for one and legal for the other because of the hypocritical way the SELP system is designed. Changing the existing SELP system is the only way to allow citizens to truly enjoy life, liberty, and the pursuit of happiness as the citizen sees fit versus as proscribed by those in power.

The alternative is to keep doing the same thing over and over again, expecting a different result. The hypocritical SELP construct is like an earlier version of the Matrix, and it is inevitable that eventually, the system will fail. The failure will occur when the twenty-trillion-dollar (and exponentially growing) US federal government debt bubble bursts.

Don't you think that the US federal government debt bubble will burst? Ask yourself this question: What do the 1929 crash and the S&L crisis in the 1970s, the crash of 1987, the dot-com crash of 2000, the Enron crash, and the combo subprime loan and fraudulent bond marketing crash all have in common? The answer is that the government and financial leaders all thought the same thing you are thinking now: It will never happen. None of them ever saw it coming!

Civil Asset Forfeiture and Economic Eminent Domain

First, the state made illegal, noninjuring-to-others activities that humans like to choose to do, thereby making virtually all citizens illegal. Then the state developed 24-7-365 monitoring of citizens so that all the activities of humans are monitored for selective prosecution of noninjuring-to-others activities. What's left? Appropriating for the state the assets of those not directly tied into the state.

Civil asset forfeiture was created to take the ill-gotten gains of big drug lords who pay no income taxes and who made their money illegally. Now the laws are being used to confiscate cars and other properties of citizens who are mostly trying to just live the life of a human.

Eminent domain is a legal concept that allows governments to take a citizen's property for the public good, such as for building a road or a sewer system. Now the legal concept has been expanded to "economic eminent domain" whereby the trickle-down socialism of the new economic development outweighs the personal property rights of the citizen.

In both cases, the same overall concept occurs: the government takes the personal property of the citizen and the citizen has no recourse, except through expensive court-related expenses that also consume the citizen's life.

Those inside the Byzantine pineapple gain, and those outside lose out. And whether morally right or wrong, it is all legal!

Tying the Four Concepts Together

In the USA, a citizen can watch an X Games athlete attempt jumping a motorcycle forty-seven feet into the air for a vault, and that is legal for the X Games athlete to do. Or a citizen can watch people play football and see physical contact that can and does cause injury, and that is legal to do.

However, if a citizen drives a vehicle without wearing a seat belt, they can be fined or imprisoned for their personal choice because driving without wearing a seat belt is dangerous and, therefore, is illegal. And since the vehicle was used in the commission of a crime, the state can simply take the vehicle, and the citizen is screwed.

For just the top 10 prescription drugs in the USA, there are 150 million monthly prescriptions. Those are prescriptions and not the number of pills sold.

For the top 100 prescription drugs in the USA, the total amount of monthly prescriptions probably exceeds the number of citizens in the USA. Those are prescriptions and not the number of prescription pills actually sold. And those are just prescribed drugs and not over-the-counter drugs. And that doesn't include illegal drug use!

Common sense should tell one that with all the prescribed OTC and illegal drugs sold in the USA, just about every single person in the USA is drugged up on something. Common sense also should tell one that whether a drug is considered legal or illegal, it is irrelevant to individuals either responsibly or irresponsibly using the drug. It is a matter of choice.

The point is that the overall behavior of engaging in thrill-seeking or in using recreational drugs is no different behavior than the behavior followed by those who use legal drugs or those who engage in dangerous sporting activities. However, while the behavior is the same, the legality/illegality of the behavior is defined differently. Ask yourself this question: Do you really know why that is?

If a citizen gambles with their money, it used to be illegal virtually everywhere. Now there are more legal gambling options, but it is still illegal in most localities for private citizens to gamble with their money.

Gambling is a matter of placing a bet and taking the risk that the bet will pay off. This is considered illegal in localities based on a concept of moral behavior.

If a citizen puts money into the financial markets, the citizen is, in effect, gambling. The citizen is placing a bet that the financial reward of the investment will outweigh the risk that the bet will pay off. The theoretical concept is that if the stock collapses or interest rates change, the investor bears the risk and reaps the reward. Somehow, this is considered moral behavior, while gambling is considered immoral, even though the bottom-line behavior is the same.

At the same time, the politicians can rob the populace through taxation structured in a Byzantine manner that selectively rewards a few while harming others. This is what happened with TARP. The legislative, administrative, and judicial branches all agreed to cover the losses of the gamblers who placed losing bets on financial instruments. The three branches of the US government (and many other governments, which followed suit on TARP) claimed that it is legal to take taxpayer's money and bail out wealthy donors who stood to lose fortunes on bad bets. The three branches of the US government (and many other governments, which followed suit on TARP) placed their own bet that the trickle-down socialism effect would do less harm to society versus letting the bankruptcy system run its course.

The question is, Why are select gambling behaviors *legal* and other select gambling behaviors *illegal*? The answer is that the SELP system in place is structured to keep it that way.

This current SELP system is doomed to fail. Why? The potential for abuse is obvious, and the stories of system abuse continue to grow annually. Citizens are being taxed at ever-increasing rates while they see that the benefits of the ever-increasing taxation are not being delivered. Instead, the citizens see

1. ever-increasing layers of laws that are only complicating their lives, doing things like making the citizen a criminal if he disagrees with the now-instituted existence tax;

2. regulatory taxation unnecessarily increasing the citizen's cost of living;
3. criminal behavior being declared noncriminal for those with money and power by the three branches of government; and
4. common citizenship being increasingly incarcerated or having stains on their police record, which affect the ability to find gainful employment, for the same behavior being declared noncriminal for those with money and power.

This simplistic presentation points out why the class of independents is growing both in the USA and also globally. It is patently obvious to the citizens that the political parties are on the take and really don't have a plan in place to address what the citizens see as the root cause of the breakdown of the concept of law. The common people are moving away from the political parties, leaving only the hard-core political party acolytes in the political parties. The hard-core acolytes are now in control of the political parties, while the independents seek a new SELP system to address the flaws of the existing SELP systems. The problem the growing independents have is that there is currently no plan presented to the citizens for a new SELP system that they feel they can support!

To create a new SELP system that will actually achieve the originally stated four goals, one must understand why the current SELP economic systems fail to achieve the stated four goals. The explanation of why the SELP systems are doomed to fail economically is illustrated by the analysis of the taxation systems in place as well as the analysis of the inherent flaws of the needs-based welfare systems.

CHAPTER 6

Why Existing SELP Systems Are Doomed to Fail

THE SEEDS OF failure for the existing global SELP systems were sown a long time ago. It is only because of the greatly increased human population, coupled with modern technology, that the seeds sown have fully manifested themselves.

The inequities of the existing SELP systems used to be able to be buried because there were less people to manage and humans couldn't see the big picture. However, with so many people today, it is impossible for the ruling party to buy votes with corruption like they used to because there are too many votes to out-and-out buy. Also, those getting screwed by the corruption can see it occur in real time, and the ability to play back what has been said is educating people to the lies that have been told.

Until the governmental macroeconomic structure goes through an evolution that is simplified and treats citizens equally, these will be the situations prevalent today: hate-filled diatribe and clever slogans spewed back and forth between the right and the left, which may score political points and make for entertaining television. But the diatribe does nothing to solve the fundamental structural deficiencies of the existing SELP systems. Until there is a fundamental restructuring of the governmental macroeconomic structure, the current existing SELP system failures will not go away.

To create a new SELP system design for the governmental macroeconomic structure, there must be systems analysis of the existing SELP governmental macroeconomic structure first to understand why the existing failures exist. Following are analyses of the failures of the taxation system and needs-based systems.

Taxation System Failures

Death and *taxes* are stated to be the only certainties of human existence. With respect to taxes, the phrase never states that taxes are intelligently applied.

In the year 2014, the government of France advocated a 75 percent tax rate on select entities. The United Nations is advocating increased taxation in various manners. The United States government has increased taxation over the last few years. Around the globe, there is a Tea Party movement that advocates less taxes and less government. In every country, there are always a variety of taxation system changes made by those in power. Ask yourself this question: Why should any human believe that any of these changes will create a better way for the citizens of the country?

The answer is that *no one* should believe that any taxation changes will have the desired effect unless there is a provable method that the tax changes will work. The failure with the current SELP taxation systems in place and proposed to be changed is that the systems are based entirely on what University of Chicago economics professor Frank Wright termed as unknown unknowns.

University of Chicago economist Frank Wright coined a concept called unknown unknowns. This concept explains the failure of the various tax rates and the various governmental budgets that are put forth as being necessary for the management of humans. The calculations of both the tax rates and the budgets are based on economic theorems that are based on economic *unknown unknowns*. These economic unknown unknowns ultimately doom the implementation of the tax rates and budgets to systematic failure. This is epitomized in art by Neo saying to Agent Smith in the climax of the Matrix trilogy: "It was inevitable."

Let's look at some examples of this inevitability of economic unknown unknowns. The United States government issues a ten-year budget annually. This budget is based on assumptions that are unknown.

There are assumptions like

1. what the interest rate of debt issued and retired will be for each of the ten years,
2. what the annual inflation rate that occurs will be for each of the ten years,
3. what the unemployment rate that occurs will be for each of the ten years,
4. what the tax rates in effect will be for each of the ten years,
5. what the social security payments made will be for each of the ten years, and
6. what will the GNP be for each of the next ten years.

The list can continue, but the point is that each of these factors is an *unknown*. The assumptions are known, but these assumptions are known to be false. The actual rates of each of the budgetary factors are unknown unknowns. The factor details are unknown, and the future factor details are unknown. Everything is an economic unknown unknown. The failure of the governmental taxation system and, inherently, the governmental budget is inevitable.

Recent years have seen the emergence of new economic theories, such as economic theories that mathematically *prove* that negative interest rates are how governments should operate. In other words, instead of entities earning interest on money lent to the government, the entities are better off losing money lent to governments. Instead of there being a positive time value of money, there is a negative time value of money.

Citizens are told to accept these economic theories issued by those who have mathematical formulations and positions of power and the backing of powerful people to support the economic theory. The failure is that the economic theorems behind such mathematical formulations are based entirely on escalating economic unknown unknowns. The mathematical theory works on paper because the paper theory assumes away all economic unknown unknowns as not fitting the formula. Therefore, the formula is not wrong. It is the economic unknown unknowns that are wrong!

The failure is that the economic unknown unknowns are the reality of SELP existence. The proper economic formula for a new SELP design seeks to eliminate economic unknown unknowns via the logical construction of the formula instead of assuming away the economic unknown unknowns. By applying systems analysis and systems design to the construction of a macroeconomic formula, a simpler, more powerful macroeconomic formula for taxation and government can be created.

The Inherent Flaws of Needs-Based Social Welfare Programs

Governments have tons of social welfare programs. These social welfare programs are almost exclusively needs-based systems.

Needs-based systems are ultimately doomed to fail. This failure is evidenced by the following programmatic events that occur with respect to needs-based systems:

1. A needs-based system requires adding Byzantine layers of bureaucracy, which adds cost and inefficiencies in operation of the needs-based systems.
2. Citizens are not treated equally by needs-based systems. The needs-based system segregates citizens into different categories, rewarding some citizens at the expense of others.
3. The categories-sorting method of the needs-based system is ultimately modified over time. This modification process adds more Byzantine layers to the original needs-based system categorization process.
4. By their very nature, needs-based systems are not designed to eliminate needs. Needs-based systems perpetually require

a continuously morphing Byzantine decision rules set to continuously make decisions about needs as the political parties in charge of the governmental systems change over time. The system is therefore about perpetuation of the needs-based systems rather than needs elimination.

5. Needs-based systems do not provide 100 percent quality control. They always have the following:

   A. User fraud of individuals or cartels who seek to profit from submitting false data to receive the capital being distributed by the needs-based system.

   B. Political, capital/largesse fraud. Political parties manipulate needs-based systems for internal fraud as well as to both buy votes and repay political favors to donors of the political parties.

   C. Natural system error. Any individual's needs change over time, but the systems design of needs-based systems is not prepared to track and account for changes in the needs / lack of needs of hundreds of millions (let alone billions) of citizens. The simplest example is the needy person who wins the big capital lottery. An income-based needs system is prone to not recognize that the lottery winner theoretically no longer has a need because of a suddenly large asset base.

   D. Conflicting needs-based systems that do not account for citizens' actions as a whole with respect to the variety of needs-based systems that a government has created. Each individual needs-based system is actually a subsystem to a macroeconomic total system. The more individual subsystems are in place, the more subsystems a citizen can apply to for needs-based assistance. The more subsystems are in place, the more Byzantine the decision-making process becomes to track the citizen. The more each individual needs-based subsystem morphs over time, the more the tracking subsystems for each needs-based subsystem must morph over time to account for all the changes that have occurred. This epitomizes the Byzantine pineapple. As time moves forward, the systems become more Byzantine.

Ask yourself this question: What is sought to be accomplished by all the various needs-based systems that governments create? The answer needs to be defined in clear, specific terms rather than nebulous buzzwords.

This system's analyst perceives that the needs-based systems are what people also termed as social welfare systems. The terminology is irrelevant. What are relevant are the goals to be accomplished. At the very simplistic core, there are three basic goals that are sought by governmental needs-based systems / social welfare systems:

1. Ensure that all citizens have enough capital to exist on a daily basis.
2. Ensure that all citizens are provided basic health care. (Note: health care is not health insurance.)
3. Ensure that all citizens have an address to call home, which has the basic needs necessary for survival (heat, power, and basic appliances).

It really is that simple. Those three items really are what the majority of government programs seek to accomplish.

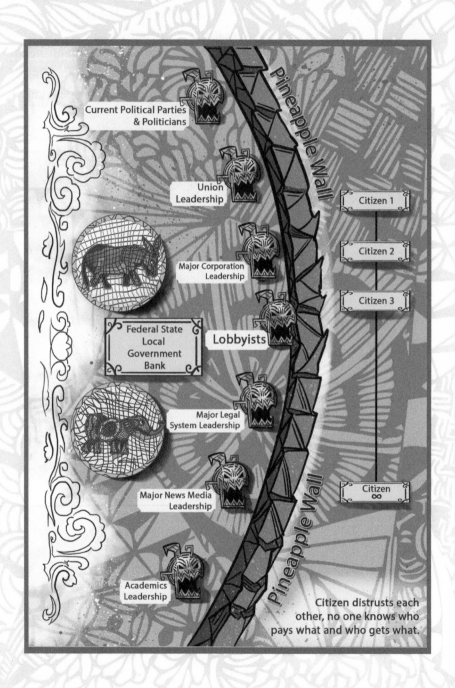

Current Political Parties & Politicians

Union Leadership

Major Corporation Leadership

Federal State Local Government Bank

Lobbyists

Major Legal System Leadership

Major News Media Leadership

Academics Leadership

Pineapple Wall

Citizen 1

Citizen 2

Citizen 3

Citizen ∞

Citizen distrusts each other, no one knows who pays what and who gets what.

PART 3

Design Parameters for Creating a New SELP System Design

CHAPTER 7

Defining Design Parameters for a New SELP System Design

TO CREATE A new SELP system, one must first establish parameters to use in establishing a new SELP system. Think about it: if one cannot clearly state the parameters of a new SELP system, then how can one know whether the desired results of a SELP System are achieved?

The following is a list of design parameters for creating a new SELP system design:

1. Use information systems' systems analysis and systems design techniques for problem-solving.
2. Eliminate as many economic unknown unknowns as possible.
3. Establish 100 percent quality control.
4. Treat citizens equally regardless of age, gender, race, ethnicity, income level, asset base, location, religion, or any other demographic factor normally used to divide citizens of a nation.
5. Establish the "keep it simple and stupid" principle (KISS principle) wherever possible.
6. Eliminate (over time) all current government social welfare programs/systems and replace them with a system that addresses the primary four goals established in the introduction.
7. Tie government spending to government revenue.

The explanations of these design parameters for creating a new SELP system design are as follows:

1. *Use information systems' systems analysis and systems design techniques for problem-solving.*

Designing a new SELP system design is similar to a new information system. Designing information system is all about problem-solving. Ask yourself this question: How is a problem defined? If the problem cannot be properly defined, then the systems analysis and systems design required to solve the problem cannot be applied. However, this concept of defining the problem applies to problems as they exist on a daily basis.

The author of this text grew up in a household with a parent who continuously responded to daily stimuli by exclaiming "The world is full of problems!" or "The government is full of problems!" or "There are so many problems in the world today!" and an ad nauseam amount of ways of stating the same thing. The author experienced in life wherein other people walking around, saying "That child is a problem child" or "That person is a problem employee." The author has been beset by such stimuli, such as "Capitalism is such a problem," "Socialism is a problem," "Communism is a problem," etc. Other expressions extend to ethnic terms such as the Jewish problem, the Palestinian problem, etc. Religion is also used in this context: "Catholics are a problem" or "Islam is a problem" or on and on and on.

The entire problem statements above are actually meaningless statements because there is no tangible definition of the word *problem*. Unless the problem in each case can be defined in a tangible method, then the statements are meaningless. Ask yourself this question: How many times during the next seven days will I hear the word *problem* used, and how many times will there be a clear definition of what the *problem* actually is? Better yet, how many times in the next seven days will you hear politicians and media personalities use the word *problem* without stating any clear problem analysis or problem solution design?

Information systems' systems analysis and systems design define the term *problem* as "a gap between reality and the way that things are desired to be." Bridging the gap is the implementation plan.

This explains why current SELP systems fail with respect to legislation passed. There is never a clear definition of systems analysis, systems design, and implementation process defined with legislation passed. Instead, what is passed is cobbled together. Another set of laws is on top of other laws with no clear definition of what *problem* the new legislation is actually trying to solve!

Try reading the Affordable Care Act or other omnibus bills passed by the United States Congress and signed by the president of the United States of America. There can be no wonder why it takes a supreme court to rule on what is actually being stated in the legislative acts. The texts are convoluted and ill-defined.

The evidence that no true systems analysis and systems design work is performed on legislation can be seen with actions regarding the passage and initial attempt to repeal and replace ACA. The passage of ACA had a "cornhusker kickback" and a "Louisiana purchase," as well as a subsequent stack of regulations ten feet high. The initial ACA repeal and replace had an "Alaska purchase." If a legislative act is organized via systems analysis and systems design, then there would be no state buyouts for votes or subsequent massive regulation stack. Proper systems design that treats citizens equally would never have bribes for votes, nor would there be a need for massive subsequent regulations. The original legislation would already contain the regulations required.

The politicians and the academics declare loudly that "This is politics!" The politicians and the academics declare loudly that there is no better SELP system that can be created. Wake up from "The Matrix"! Don't fall for that Jedi mind trick! A better SELP system can be designed and implemented. What is required is to take a comprehensive view of the existing system and then designing the new system to address existing system flaws. The differences between the two models are the implementation path.

2. *Eliminate as many economic unknown unknowns as possible.*

Part 1 already documented what economic unknown unknowns are. The issue is whether the reader really understands what the impact of existing unknown unknowns baked into the existing SELP systems are and whether the reader understands how these unknown unknowns can be eliminated.

Think about this: Each year for ten years, leading up to 2009 and 2010, the US federal budget made all sorts of projections comprised of thousands of pages of unknown unknowns. Then in 2009 and 2010, the US government passed TARP, ACA, and a nearly trillion-dollar stimulus package. Logically, this means that all projections made for the prior ten years leading up to 2009 and 2010 were essentially junk. The budgets didn't account for the massive spending of these programs!

Similarly, the budgets of 2009 and 2010 and in subsequent years ended up being junk. Those budgets were based on expected results of the legislation of TARP, ACA, and a nearly trillion-dollar stimulus package passed, but those expectations were actually unknown unknowns that never came to fruition.

This process of governments passing useless budgets based on unknown unknowns–based projections occurs annually at every level of government in each governing authority around the globe. These budgets are essentially junk because they will never come close to being a reality.

The definition of *insanity* is "doing the same thing over and over again, expecting a different result." Continuing to create and pass junk budgets over and over again and expecting problems to be resolved is insane.

3. *Establish 100 percent quality control.*

After World War II, an American statistician named William Edward Deming went to Japan to assist in the industrial reconstruction of Japan. The Deming Prize that carries his name is such a prestigious award that Japanese television annually broadcasts the award presentation.

Dr. Deming would hold seminars on quality control where statistical analysis of errors would be calculated via a simple example. A bowl full of mostly white but with scattered red balls would be brought forth. A paddle would be inserted into the bowl, and the seminar attendees would mathematically calculate the error rate of production as noted by the amount of red (error) balls withdrawn from the bowl.

After a series of calculations that mathematically prove the error rate, Dr. Deming would, in essence, inform the seminar attendees that they have wasted their time. The reason that the time is wasted is that for all the mathematical calculations performed, not one single step has been taken to prevent red balls from entering the bowl. The errors still occur.

The needs-based systems in place are all designed to *inject* red balls into the system. Continuing to use flawed needs-based systems while expecting these systems to work to solve problems is insane.

In other words, it is a waste of time to design a system that allows for quality defects and then spend time documenting the error rate. The inherent system problems are *not* being solved. Hence, 100 percent quality control is a design parameter of a new SELP system.

4. *Treat citizens equally regardless of age, gender, race, ethnicity, income level, asset base, location, religion, or any other demographic factor normally used to divide citizens of a nation.*

The United States of America's Declaration of Independence states, "We hold these truths to be self-evident, that all men [people] are created equal, that they are endowed by their Creator with certain unalienable Rights, that among these are Life, Liberty and the Pursuit of Happiness."

This statement contains a parameter of systems design. The parameter is a systems design that treats people equally while allowing for life, liberty, and the pursuit of happiness.

One of the biggest contributors to hate is distrust. One of the greatest sowers of distrust is the existing SELP systems. This is because the existing SELP systems establish parameters of treating citizens differently depending on who the citizen is. Rather than treating citizens equally because the citizens are citizens with equal rights, the existing SELP systems segregate citizens into thousands of different classes and then allot government resources based on the thousands of different classes established by the government.

What is the result of all the subclassifying of the citizenship? Distrust, because those who pay more and get less of the Byzantine pineapple dole or who perceive they pay more and get less distrust the government and those receiving more and paying less or who are perceived to be receiving more and paying less. Those actually paying less and receiving more also don't want the gravy train to end, and they promote distrust by deflecting citizens to other perceived injustices except the ones that they themselves are committing.

The purpose of the government shouldn't be segregating and pitting the citizenship against one another. The purpose of the government should be to treat the citizenship equally.

5. *Establish the "keep it simple and stupid" principle (KISS principle) wherever possible.*

Currently in the United States, there is a constant push to pass more and more laws via massive omnibus bills that aren't really being read or debated before being voted upon. This epitomizes how the US government is operating in an anti-KISS-principle manner.

The new SELP system needs to reestablish a simpler citizen-to-government relationship. This can be done by defining a simpler database relationship of citizen to government. There should be no need for each government department to have multiple databases carrying redundant citizen data. Instead, there should be a single department of information systems that feeds the functions of government, thereby simplifying the citizen-to-government relationship.

6. *Eliminate (over time) all current government social welfare programs/systems and replace them with a system that addresses the four primary goals established in the introduction.*

As already noted in the text, there are hundreds of US federal government needs-based programs all designed to actually accomplish three primary tasks:

1. Provide an income to each citizen.
2. Provide health care (not health insurance) to each citizen.
3. Provide some form of housing to each citizen.

Also, already noted is that needs-based programs are doomed to never accomplish the stated program goals due to inherent system flaws. Ergo, a new SELP system needs to eliminate (in an orderly methodical manner over time) existing needs-based systems and replace these systems with simpler KISS-adhering programs.

7. *Tie government spending to government revenue.*

The only way to stop current politicians from sending future generations further in debt is to construct a SELP system that balances government spending to government revenue. It's called living within your means.

There is another aspect to think about. For the United States federal government (and many other federal governments around the globe), no political parties have a macroeconomic plan that balances government revenue to government spending. Inherently, this means that none of the political parties really value this idea.

CHAPTER 8

A New SELP System Design

THE NEW SELP macroeconomic system that meets the goals and parameters are defined herein.

The following is a construct of a new SELP systems design that fits the parameters previously outlined:

A. Use tax subrates to prebudget government departments.

B. Sum up the tax rates to come to a flat tax rate applied to all citizens.

C. Force all benefits for government workers to a 401(k)-style plan.

D. Eliminate all health insurance (over time) and just have the government pay for the citizens' health-care bills out of a new health-care tax subrate.

E. Eliminate all government programs (over time) that pay anything for citizens based on need. Establish a new monthly payment for all citizens with the same monthly government stipend regardless of any factors, such as age, race, asset base, income level, etc. The stipend is established by a new stipend tax subrate.

F. Eliminate all government housing programs (over time). Establish government housing areas where any citizens can go live if they so desire. The zones are paid for by a new tax subrate.

The following text expands upon these system design parameters:

A. *Use tax subrates to prebudget government departments.*

Ask yourself this question: Why *must* governments be funded by forms of appropriation bills? The answer is that there is no *must*. How government departments are funded is a matter of choice.

The failure of existing SELP systems—a failure that has been proven again and again throughout history—is that without spending control on those in power, they will continue to increase taxes and government spending to the point of bankrupting the country. The way to accomplish control is to prebudget government with taxation that is directly tied to government spending.

The way to prebudget government via taxation is to use tax subrates for each government department. This is best illustrated for understanding by using a direct example.

The following page contains the US federal budget for 2013 as per Wikipedia. The second page shows each department's budgeted percentage as a percentage of the PTD. Whether these pages ended up being the exact budget is irrelevant for the purposes of illustration. The total percentage of department is listed as well as the total percentage of all spending that each department accounts for.

The totals column is ultimately a percentage of the total annual population of tax dollars (PTD). Assume that the PTD for the US federal budget for 2013 was $9 trillion. The military's budget of $672.9 billion for the year was 7.3 percent of the PTD. Therefore, the subrate for the military is 7.3 percent.

Applying the same logic to all the US governmental departments provides the result on page 49.

Agency	Discretionary	Mandatory	Total	% of Total
Department of Defense including Overseas Contingency Operations	666	6.7	672.9	17.7%
Department of Health and Human Services including Medicare and Medicaid	80.6	860.3	940.9	24.7%
Department of Education	67.7	4.2	71.9	1.9%
Department of Veterans Affairs	60.4	79.4	139.7	3.7%
Department of Housing and Urban Development	41.1	5.2	46.3	1.2%
Department of State and Other International Programs	56.1	3.4	59.5	1.6%
Department of Homeland Security	54.9	0.5	55.4	1.5%
Department of Energy	35.6	−0.6	35.0	0.9%
Department of Justice	23.9	12.7	36.5	1.0%
Department of Agriculture	26.8	127.7	154.5	4.1%
National Aeronautics and Space Administration	17.8	−0.02	17.8	0.5%
National Intelligence Program	52.6	0	52.6	1.4%
Department of Transportation	24.0	74.5	98.5	2.6%
Department of the Treasury	14.1	96.2	110.3	2.9%
Department of the Interior	12.3	1.2	13.5	0.4%
Department of Labor	13.2	88.4	101.7	2.7%
Social Security Administration	11.7	871.0	882.7	23.2%
Department of Commerce	9.5	−0.5	9.0	0.2%
Army Corps of Engineers Civil Works	8.2	−0.007	8.2	0.2%
Environmental Protection Agency	9.2	−0.2	8.9	0.2%
National Science Foundation	7.4	0.2	7.5	0.2%
Small Business Administration	1.4	−0.006	1.4	0.0%
Corporation for National and Community Service	1.1	0.007	1.1	0.0%
Net interest	0	246	246	6.5%
Disaster costs	2	0	2	0.0%
Other spending	34.0-	61.7	29.5	0.8%
Total	**1,264**	**2,539**	**3,803**	

M% is defined as the % of PTD dedicated to fund military = $672.9B   7.3%

E% is defined as the % of PTD dedicated to fund education = $72B   0.80%

VA% is defined as the % of PTD dedicated to fund Veteran Affairs = $140B   1.55%

ST% is defined as the % of PTD dedicated to fund the State Department = $60B   0.66%

DHS% is defined as the % of PTD dedicated to fund the Department of Homeland Security = $56B   0.62%

EY% is defined as the % of PTD dedicated to fund the Energy Department = $56B   0.62%

J% is defined as the % of PTD dedicated to fund the Justice Department = $37B   0.41%

A% is defined as the % of PTD dedicated to fund agriculture = $154B   1.71%

N% is defined as the % of PTD dedicated to fund NASA = $18B   0.20%

NIP% is defined as the % of PTD dedicated to fund the National Intelligence Program = $52B   0.58%

T% is defined as the % of PTD dedicated to fund transportation = $98B   1.08%

TRE% is defined as the % of PTD dedicated to fund the Department of Treasury = $110B   1.22%

INTER% is defined as the % of PTD dedicated to Fund the Department of Interior = $13.5B   0.15%

LBR% is defined as the % of PTD dedicated to fund the Department of Labor = $102B   1.13%

CE% is defined as the % of PTD dedicated to fund the Commerce Department = $9B   0.10%

ACE% is defined as the % of PTD dedicated to fund the Army Corps Engineers = $8B   0.09%

EPA % is defined as the % of PTD dedicated to fund the EPA = $9B   0.10%

CNS% is defined as the % of PTD dedicated to fund the National Science Foundation = $8B   0.09%

SB% is defined as the % of PTD dedicated to fund the Small Business ADM = $1.4B   0.01%

NSF% is defined as the % of PTD dedicated to fund the Corp. for Nat'l Service = $1.1B   0.01%

IS% is defined as the % of PTD dedicated to fund a proposed Department of Information Systems = TBD

Total All Subrates   18.43%

This 18.43 percent is the basis for a flat tax. However, there are more items to be addressed, namely, needs-based programs, which also tie back to government department budgeting.

With respect to a government department budget, there are four categories of expenditures:

1. Current labor obligations (payroll, payroll taxes, 401(k), etc.)
2. Future labor obligations (pension, disability, etc.)
3. Operations expenses
4. Capital program expenses

Items 1, 3, and 4 can be fixed in value, which makes these expenditures *known*. It is the second category of future labor obligations that is an *unknown unknown*. By grandfathering out all future labor obligations to be handled in a different manner, the budgets for the departments shrink. The way to handle the future labor operations moving forward is resolved by the way that current needs-based programs are grandfathered out and replaced with a much simpler system. How this is accomplished is explained as the text proceeds.

B. *Force all benefits for government workers to a 401(k)-style plan.*

Pension plans are 100 percent unknown unknowns. The *401(k)* plans are known. The unknown unknown needs to be 100 percent replaced with the known for *all* government employees.

C. *Eliminate all health insurance (over time) and have the government pay citizens' health-care bills out of a new health-care tax subrate.*

Insurance is a product of pooled risk to pay out a benefit if an incident occurs. But if the public opinion and direction is that all citizens are provided health care, then why is there a need for health insurance?

Another way of phrasing this is that if citizens are mandated to buy health insurance plans that do not cover 100 percent of the possible medical issues that a citizen may need health care for, then there is no 100 percent quality control. If the goal is to provide health care yet the mandated insurance doesn't cover the expenses of the health care required, then what use is the health insurance?

The fact is that there actually is no need for a health insurance system for citizens. The expenditures can be billed to and paid for by the federal government. This dramatically brings costs down because all the systems required to support Byzantine payment and remittance systems, as well as paying large salary amounts to an eliminated industry, will be eliminated.

The phase in plan would be to start with dental services. A definition of the annual services (such as annual teeth cleaning) as well as the base-covered cost for dental procedures is required. For example, if a citizen destroys his/her teeth because he/she is a crystal meth user, then the citizen gets a new set of base teeth to provide health care to the citizen. If the citizen is capable of affording and wants a better set of replacement teeth, then the citizen can pay the difference between the base set and the final set.

Using such a system to start would allow the bugs to be worked out of such a system, and then the system can be expanded to cancer treatments, AIDS treatments, etc. Eventually, a stasis occurs, and all citizens have 100 percent health care.

With respect to the government departments' future benefits for medical, there simply is no need for department budgets to carry the costs. The medical insurance costs (and administrative costs) would also disappear from the corporate world, increasing profits and allowing for a greater PTD annually. All medical cost bankruptcies would vanish over time.

Using the 2013 health and human services budget as a proxy, the expenditure is $940 billion. This works out to a 10.44 percent value for a subrate labeled H percent.

D. *Eliminate all government programs (over time) that pay anything for citizens based on need. Establish a new equal monthly payment to all citizens. The stipend is established by a new stipend tax subrate.*

Common sense dictates that all citizens need capital to survive. But as the text has already shown, the needs-based system of allocating capital to citizens is flawed. How to replace the needs-based systems with a system that achieves the stated SELP system goals of treating citizens equally as well as following the KISS principle is the question.

The solution is to establish a tax subrate that gathers funds that are redistributed monthly to citizens in an equal amount regardless of age, race, gender, income, asset base, or any other factor. The monthly amount distributed to each citizen will not be a significant amount but will be enough to live off because of the following:

A. As the prior section noted, the citizen will not be subjected to expenses related to health care.
B. As the subsequent section notes, a tax subrate to provide paid-for living to any citizen who desires it can be established.

Without anyone having to pay for health or shelter expenses, a citizen can exist on a nominal stipend each month. Other citizens also know that when an individual or family is seeking assistance, the basic needs of the individual or family are already taken care of.

Inherently, this means grandfathering out the Social Security System because a citizen can always decide to save or not to save for the future, but that is a moot point. The citizen's needs are taken care of monthly in a KISS-principle manner.

This also means the elimination of the unemployment tax system as well as many other federal systems. Since citizens are already receiving a monthly stipend and can receive health care and can move into a housing zone if necessary, then there is no need for mass quantities of disparate government programs.

The concept of "too big to fail" is no longer relevant. If a corporation fails and citizens lose jobs, that is a tragedy. But the needs of the citizens are automatically covered, so there is no need for government involvement in performing trickle-down socialism to prop up failing corporations.

Assume that there are three hundred million citizens and the target value sought is to redistribute $1 trillion annually. This works out to $278/month to each citizen or approximately $65/week. Based on a $9 trillion PTD, this works out to a flat tax rate of 11.11 percent.

Those in larger cities will argue that such an equal distribution is unfair to them because the cost of living in their locality is greater. This is a false argument because of the following:

1. If it is possible to define the locations of the greater economic costs, it is possible to define the government(s) in charge of the greater economic cost.
2. There is nothing precluding the region/government(s) of the greater economic area from also collecting and redistributing local income in the same manner to the local citizens, thereby supplementing the federal stipend.

In other words, any difference in economic value is a local issue. It is the role of the federal government to treat citizens equally.

The payment system for each citizen can be established and managed by a new federal department of information systems. To qualify for a monthly benefit, citizens must annually certify their existence in person with the new federal department of information systems. At the same time, such items as voter registration can also be taken care of, thereby eliminating the perpetual angst over the registered voter issue.

C. *Eliminate all government housing programs (over time). Establish government housing areas where any citizen can go live if the citizen so desires. The zones are paid for by a new tax subrate.*

If citizens want a place to live, they can't just go into the wilderness and build their own home from scratch. There are too many humans on earth, and all the properties are owned by some entity. The choices are to own or to rent or to live free with others, or else, some other accommodations are made.

Current SELP systems have evolved systems to provide housing to the needy, but the same issues that plague all need-based systems are built into the existing SELP systems. The existing systems are too costly as well as fraud filled.

The KISS system solution is that the government must provide basic housing with basic utilities to any citizen who wants to exist in such a basic lifestyle. The government pays the utility and maintenance costs, and the payment for such housing is paid for out of another tax subrate to pay for the housing.

The federal allocation per citizen should be in an equal amount per person. If localities feel that the local economics require more funding per citizen, then, as with the monthly stipend, the local government for a defined area can supplement the federal payment.

Other Subrates Required to Balance Out the US Model

There are three other subrates required for the US model:

A. A factor to balance out the grandfathering out of the existing Social Security System. The theory is that the Social Security System should balance itself out. The reality is probably something different, and this points out the flaws inherent in the existing Social Security System.
B. A factor for paying the annual interest amount due for the national debt.
C. A factor for paying down at least some of the national debt principal.

The Base Macroeconomic Formula

The summation macroeconomic formula of the flat tax plan is the following:

Flat Tax Rate % = (S%) + (SS%) + (H%) + (L%) + (D%) + (I%) + (M%) + (E%) + (VA%) + (ST%) + (DHS%) + (EY%) + (J%) + (A%) + (N%) + (NIP%) + (T%) + (TRE%) + (INTER%) + (LBR%) + (CE%) + (ACE%) + (EPA%) + (NSF%) + (SB%)+ (CNS%) + (IS%)

Note: The full definitions of each % is in appendix A on page 67.

Using the already noted percentages, the calculated rate is as follows:

Flat Tax Rate % = (11.11%) + (0%) + (10.44%) + (5.55%) + (TBD) + (2.73%) + (7.3%) + (.80%) + (1.55%) + (0.66%) + (0.62%) + (0.62%) + (0.41%) + (1.71%) + (0.2%) + (0.58%) + (1.08%) + (1.22%) + (0.15%) + (1.13%) + (0.10%) + (0.09%) + (0.10%) + (0.09%) + (0.01%) + (0.01%) + (TBD%) = 48.26% plus TBD

While this amount seems excessive, the final actual rate should be less than the value shown in this model. Why? There are three reasons:

1. Incomes rise as existing costs are eliminated so the percentage of population of tax dollars required for the same funding level decreases.
2. There is existing taxation that will vanish.
3. Citizens can change the rates.

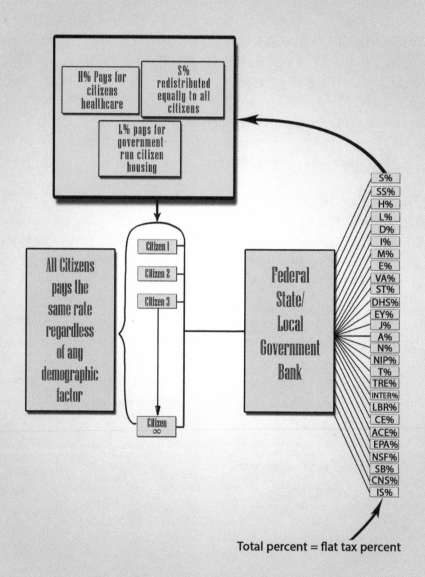

Citizen trust each other because they know everyone is treated equally.

H% Pays for citizens healthcare

S% redistributed equally to all citizens

L% pays for government-run citizen housing

All Citizens pays the same rate regardless of any demographic factor

Citizen 1

Citizen 2

Citizen 3

Citizen ∞

Federal State/ Local Government Bank

S%
SS%
H%
L%
D%
I%
M%
E%
VA%
ST%
DHS%
EY%
J%
A%
N%
NIP%
T%
TRE%
INTER%
LBR%
CE%
ACE%
EPA%
NSF%
SB%
CNS%
IS%

Total percent = flat tax percent

Incomes rise as existing costs are eliminated so the percentage of population of tax dollars required for the same funding level decreases.

The operations of corporations become more profitable due to the elimination of the medical costs from corporations. The direct expense (paying health insurance premiums) and indirect experience (staff, legal, etc.) to support the HR systems will vanish over time as the plan is implemented.

Assume that this is a 10 percent increase in the PTD. This increases PTD from $9 trillion to $9.9 trillion. Under the $9 trillion example, the rate is 48.26 percent in the hypothetical model equal to $4.34 trillion in taxes collected. If the PTD is now $9.9 trillion, then the aggregate required to fund the same $4.34 trillion is now 43.87 percent for a 4.39 percent decrease.

A 20 percent PTD increase would drop the rate to 40.22 percent for an 8.04 percent reduction.

There is existing taxation that will vanish.

There is no accounting in the model for taxation that disappears. The following list is just a few of the major explanations of what that statement means:

1. There is no longer an unemployment system and unemployment taxation. The expense of such a system will disappear (lowering the departmental taxation rate subrate), and paychecks will increase as citizens are no longer paying this tax.
2. Corporate expenses are lessened as the massive amount of human resource work required for medical insurance disappears as the direct health-care system is built and insurance is phased out. Profits are up, which means there is more income to be taxed.
3. With the elimination of the health insurance system over time, the expenses for medical should drop. All the money paid to support a complex Byzantine insurance system simply vanish by

a simpler, more streamlined system. Also, employee paychecks increase because federal insurance system taxes are eliminated.

4. Since the federal government is prebudgeted, then spending pork barrel via buying votes to pass an appropriation bill goes away. The legislative branch can't get money for programs by holding spending bills hostage for pork barrel projects to buy the votes of the politicians.

5. The current focus of government departments is to spend 100 percent of the current year budget so that the next year will see an increase in budget money to spend. Prebudgeting the government means that there now becomes a focus to more effectively use the budgetary dollars available, because when the current year's funding runs out, then the department is shut down until the next year. Plus, capital purchases for a department must be planned out, so there is now a need to build a departmental cash reserve to be able to invest in major new projects.

6. All the tax dollars spent to support various special interests are minimized because there is simply no need for the government to spend money on the special interests. Since all citizens have no immediate financial need for base-living expense or medical or housing, then there is no need to have government money spent on stimulus, jobs programs, etc. The responsibility shifts away from the current trickle-down socialism construct to a free-market construct.

These are but a few of the anticipated tax reductions of a simpler flat tax system that ties government spending to government revenue via a fixed tax subrate system. The point is that the final rate can be expected to be a lot less than the 48 percent calculated using the existing budgets.

Citizens can change the rates.

A method of citizen-approved rate changes must be built into the SELP system. System evolution must be built into the system construct.

Consider how this SELP system would function versus the existing United States system. Currently, every time the military wants a new program or some special interest wants more money to fight for a cause, then funding is achieved by an act of congress. This process is lumped together with other funding requests in the bill, and eventually, enough votes are cobbled together for approval. There is no real accountability for what eventually happens.

With the subrate system described, the US military gets 7.3 percent. If the military wants a new program, then the funding is either achievable within the 7.3 percent or the funding isn't achievable. If the military makes the case that the 7.3 percent is not enough to fund current operations while also planning for future programs, then the military can petition to have the rate changed to a higher rate. The issue is that there is now an emphasis on future planning within the context of a fixed budgetary amount.

In the case of a new military operation à la desert storm or desert swarm, the military can either afford the operations within the context of the 7.3 percent or the military can petition the citizens for a new tax subrate that is designed to pay for the operation. This new subrate provides visibility to the citizens that this specific subrate of the flat tax is funding the operation, and as the operation winds down, the subrate should reduce and disappear.

The same logic is true for events such as the next Ebola or Zika or other scares plastered across news media that are used to argue that more money is needed to combat the scary, new potential pandemic. Either the funding is already available or an added subrate is needed.

Obviously, the primary subrate for a department can be broken down further. Continuing the example, the 7.3 percent for the US military can be broken down further into US Army, Air Force, Navy, Marines, Coast Guard, and what other designations required to sum up to the 7.3 percent.

The following are other benefits to society by this form of SELP system:

A. The angst in society over homeless or medical bankruptcies or other social issues goes away because there is a "100 percent coverage for all the citizens of the country." When citizens see panhandlers, they can know with 100 percent assuredness that there is no direct reason for the panhandlers to be seeking money.

B. Every week and every month, there is hoopla over government reports about jobs and unemployment. While the reporting will still go on, the hoopla will go away because there is simply no need for it. Who cares how many people are employed? The issue is that citizens are 100 percent taken care of for the basics of life.

C. Citizens know where their tax dollars are going versus the current fungible system where money appropriated for one purpose is suddenly used for a completely different purpose.

D. For situations such as violence against women, there is a clearly defined residence where the woman can go and live.

E. For convicts released from prison, there is a clearly defined place to live and an income to exist off. This can minimize crime as society will be less tolerant for thieving, so there is no need for thieving.

F. Social diseases such as sexually transmitted diseases should be easier to treat and control. Why? Because there are no financial or administrative procedural issues other than proof of citizenship to getting both diagnosis and treatment.

There are a plethora of other benefits, such as a simplified KISS principle, that the SELP system should provide. The concept is that the citizenship is working together toward a common SELP structure that any citizen in the modern world should be able to rapidly understand.

THE CHOICE IS ALWAYS YOURS TO MAKE!

BYZANTINE SYSTEM	SIMPLIFIED SYSTEM
A SYSTEM BASED UPON UNKNOWN UNKNOWNS	A SYSTEM BASED UPON KNOWNS
BIAS BASED SYSTEM	EQUALITY BASED SYSTEM
CONTINUOUS CRISIS SYSTEM	PLANNED PLACID SYSTEM
SYSTEM THAT PROMOTES FRAUD OPPORTUNITIES	SYSTEM MINIMIZING FRAUD
SYSTEM THAT CREATES FEDERAL DEFICITS	SYSTEM BALANCING THE BUDGET
SYSTEM THAT NEVER SOLVES CITIZEN NEEDS FOR A) PERSONAL INCOME B) HEALTH CARE C) ADDRESSING HOMELESSNESS	SYSTEM COVERING ALL 3 NEEDS 100%
SYSTEM THAT PROMOTES VIOLENCE & HATRED	SYSTEM PROMOTING PEACE AND EQUALITY

CHAPTER 9

Conclusion

THE SELP SYSTEM described in this text are as follows:

1. It is not an "overnight" solution. Implementation requires the populace to buy off that this solution is to be implemented over a multiyear period.
2. It treats all citizens equally regardless of any demographic factors, such as age, race, religion, ethnicity, etc.
3. It places importance upon being a citizen and requires that all humans within a country, either a citizen or else, have some form of SELP system designation (work visa and others). The benefits provided to noncitizens depend on the SELP system designation of the noncitizen.
4. It provides for 100 percent coverage of all citizens' basic needs of food, shelter, and health care.
5. It is designed for a nonviolent transition from existing SELP systems to this new SELP system.

Some people will cry "This is Socialism!" Look back at the current US budgets %'s documented in this text. The Military only accounts for 7.3% of the budget. The rest of the 92.7% is arguably going to fund Socialism! The money is already being spent. It just isn't being spent in an equitable and cost effective manner.

Ask yourself this question the next time you hear a politician or a news pundit speaking about legislation proposed to solve some societal problem: Will the legislation cost-effectively deliver 100 percent coverage for the citizens as described by the SELP system described in this text?

The author of this text can state with 100 percent certainty that unless the legislation is actually designed as described in this text, the legislation will fail. Some parties inside the Byzantine pineapple reap the benefits, and those outside the Byzantine pineapple get the shaft.

The definition of *insanity* is "performing the same actions over and over and over again, expecting a different result." To abscond with a marketing phrase and a movie tagline used in the past, it is time to stop the insanity and to wake up from "The Matrix"!

To show your support for *The Byzantine Pineapple* please visit www. poje.biz and sign up for the Quarterly Corporation X Newsletter. The more people who sign up because they see the concepts proposed the greater the power to build the New Construct!

Definitions of the Flat Tax Formula

Economic Unknown Unknowns of the Flat Tax Formula

S% is defined as the percentage of PTD dedicated to fund a universally equal redistribution of wealth to all citizens.

SS% is defined as the percentage of PTD required to resolve all current outstanding Social Security obligations as the system is phased out. In theory, this should be 0 percent for the program is designed to pay for itself.

H% is defined as the percentage of PTD required for health care of citizens.

L% is defined as the percentage of PTD dedicated to paying for living quarters for citizens who opt for the public housing zone option.

Economic Knowns of the Flat Tax Formula

I% is defined as the percentage of PTD required to make interest payments on the US debt.

D% is defined as the percentage of PTD required to pay down a portion of the US debt.

M% is defined as the percentage of PTD used to fund the military department.

E% is defined as the percentage of PTD dedicated to fund education.

VA% is defined as the percentage of PTD dedicated to fund Veteran Affairs.

ST% is defined as the percentage of PTD dedicated to fund the State Department.

DHS% is defined as the percentage of PTD dedicated to fund the Department of Homeland Security.

EY% is defined as the percentage of PTD dedicated to fund the Department of Energy.

J% is defined as the percentage of PTD dedicated to fund the Justice Department.

A% is defined as the percentage of PTD dedicated to fund agriculture.

N% is defined as the percentage of PTD dedicated to fund NASA.

NIP% is defined as the percentage of PTD dedicated to fund National Intelligence Program.

T% is defined as the percentage of PTD dedicated to fund transportation.

TRE% is defined as the percentage of PTD dedicated to fund the Department of Treasury.

INTER% is defined as the percentage of PTD dedicated to fund the Department of Interior.

LBR% is defined as the percentage of PTD dedicated to fund the Department of Labor.

CE% is defined as the percentage of PTD dedicated to the Commerce Department.

ACE% is defined as the percentage of PTD dedicated to fund the Army Corps of Engineers.

INTER% is defined as the percentage of PTD dedicated to fund the Department of Interior.

EPA% is defined as the percentage of PTD dedicated to fund the Environmental Protection Agency.

NSF% is defined as the percentage of PTD dedicated to fund the National Science Foundation.

SB% is defined as the percentage of PTD dedicated to fund the Small Business Administration.

CNS% is defined as the percentage of PTD dedicated to fund the Corps for National Service.

IS% is defined as the percentage of PTD dedicated to fund the Department of Information Systems.